Who Is Happy?

A BOOK ABOUT EMOTIONS

BY NICK REBMAN

The Child's World
childsworld.com

Published by The Child's World®
1980 Lookout Drive • Mankato, MN 56003-1705
800-599-READ • www.childsworld.com

Acknowledgments
The Child's World®: Mary Swensen, Publishing Director
Red Line Editorial: Editorial direction and production
The Design Lab: Design

Photographs ©: Shutterstock Images, cover (top left), cover
(top middle), cover (middle left), 10, 11; Vikram Raghuvanshi/
iStockphoto, cover (top right); Maxim Ibragimov/Shutterstock
Images, cover (middle right); iStockphoto, cover (bottom left);
Dmitry Kalinovsky/Shutterstock Images, cover (bottom middle);
Jani Bryson/iStockphoto, cover (bottom right); Sergey Novikov/
Shutterstock Images, 4; Suzanne Tucker/Shutterstock Images, 5;
Federico Rostagno/Shutterstock Images, 6; Dmytro Gilitukha/
Shutterstock Images, 7; Martin Novak/Shutterstock Images, 8,
9; Blend Images/Shutterstock Images, 12–13

ISBN 9781503807679
LCCN 2015958121

Printed in the United States of America
Mankato, MN
June, 2016
PA02306

About the Author

Nick Rebman likes to write, draw, and travel. He lives in Minnesota.

Everyone has feelings.
Can you match the right
person to each feeling?

Two teams play a baseball game.
Ben is on the team that wins.
Paul is on the team that loses.

Who is feeling happy?

Mom takes Jim and Amy to the candy shop. Mom says Jim can get a piece of candy. Mom says Amy cannot get one.

Who
is feeling
sad?

Two sisters play outside.
They sit on a bench. Eva
calls Sarah a mean name.

Who is feeling angry?

Emma goes to art class. She has yellow paint on her hands. Mia and Kate wipe paint on her face.

Who is feeling surprised?

Three kids sit on a park bench. Leah and Megan are telling jokes. They will not talk to Victor.

Who is feeling lonely?

ANSWER KEY

Ben is happy.
Amy is sad.
Sarah is angry.
Emma is surprised.
Victor is lonely.

GLOSSARY

angry (AN-gree) An angry person is upset or annoyed. Sarah felt angry.

happy (HAP-ee) A happy person is pleased or glad. Ben felt happy.

lonely (LONE-lee) A lonely person is sad because he or she is apart from other people. Victor felt lonely.

sad (SAD) A sad person is unhappy. Amy felt sad.

surprised (sur-PRIZED) A surprised person has something unexpected happen to him or her. Emma felt surprised.

TO LEARN MORE

IN THE LIBRARY

Llenas, Anna. *The Color Monster: A Pop-Up Book of Feelings*.
New York: Sterling Children's Books, 2015.

Millar, Goldie and Lisa A. Berger. *F Is For Feelings*.
Minneapolis, MN: Free Spirit Publishing, 2014.

Witek, Jo. *In My Heart: A Book of Feelings*. New York: Abrams, 2014.

ON THE WEB

Visit our Web site for links about emotions: childsworld.com/links

Note to Parents, Teachers, and Librarians: We routinely verify our Web links to make sure they are safe and active sites. So encourage your readers to check them out!

INDEX